NO SHORTCUTS
to
VICTORY

LARRY GEIGLE

COACHBEAR
BOOKS

TABLE OF CONTENTS

INTRODUCTION

After over forty years of playing, observing, and coaching, I thought I might pass on some thoughts about coaching and how I view football and the other games I've played.

Honestly, I wanted to write this stuff down so that I have a record of my great coaching memories. My wife says I live in the past, and I say why not? The past was exciting, and packed full of wonderful moments. And the benefit of reading about philosophies from years ago is that they've been tested over time, and they *work*.

This book will help you become a better coach or player. Even if you learn just one new idea from it, it will be worth the read. I'm sure you will find my ideas and philosophies helpful, especially if you're new to playing or coaching. And if you've been involved with sports for a while, my ideas might refresh what you already know. Everything I have written here is first-hand information that comes from my many hours and years as a coach. Use what you can and remember that time is your best friend in becoming a great coach.

Thanks for reading *No Shortcuts to Victory*.

HONORING COACHES

No Shortcuts to Victory summarizes and shares lessons learned from years of coaching. This includes the importance of player accountability and performance in practice as well as games. I try to provide you with a better understanding of how many hours it takes for coaches to develop their players so they can compete at a higher level. *No Shortcuts to Victory* discusses time-tested philosophies on head coaching, character building, and sportsmanship. It honors coaches who build athletic programs in their communities, dedicating their time and effort to America's greatest games. It also honors coaches who are coaching for the right reasons and setting a good example for young players.

I hope you enjoy the lessons learned in *No Shortcuts to Victory*. Thanks for your time!

MY FIRST HEAD COACHING POSITION

After graduating from college, my first coaching position was at Highland Park Middle School in Beaverton, Oregon. I was the head football coach.

I had no experience, so you can imagine how nervous I was. I immediately started thinking about what offense and defense I would use and who my assistant coaches would be. I wanted to know where our strengths were and where we needed help. It was important that we worked together as a staff, sharing our ideas and respecting each other's input. As coaches, we needed to be knowledgeable and bring positive energy while being excited about coaching football. We needed to be tough, and we needed to be worthy of our players' faith and respect.

As the head coach, I was hired to take the program in a good direction and earn the respect of my young players as well as the other coaches. There's nothing worse than when a coach won't delegate responsibility, as happens when assistant coaches won't let the head coach do his job. When everyone wants to do it *their* way, they steal authority from the person who needs it the most.

Remember this: there can be only one head coach, and he always has the final say. The head coach needs to coach his style of offense, defense, and special teams—a style that he understands and believes in. There's nothing wrong with trying something new, but new ideas need to be well thought-out and used for a good reason, and then practiced and implemented at the appropriate time. It takes time to develop and assimilate a new offense or defense before running it. Change can sometimes draw a coach out of his mindset, both complicating and weakening the program.

I wanted to make sure that the parents of my players knew we were taking good care of their young athletes, and that we were together as a team. We wanted to teach the right attitudes to help them become successful at winning football games. But most importantly, we wanted them to become winners in their daily lives. We needed to walk our talk and be good examples for them to be around.

These observations are not only valuable for athletic teams, but for the workplace as well.

COACH SETS THE PACE

Last summer, I was sitting in the bleachers at Mountainside High School, in Beaverton, Oregon. I was watching the new football coach, Coach Mannion, run his players through their practice. I was there to support my grandson, Landon Sherman, in his attempt to make the varsity team. I had watched Landon through the years, starting when he was just a little guy. From the moment he started playing, he loved the game of football and enjoyed competing and being part of a team.

Sitting there, I watched as Coach Mannion pushed his players to work hard; putting pressure on them to break from the huddle, run up to the line of scrimmage, and then quickly hike the football. He was teaching his players that doing things at a faster tempo creates a winning edge, helps with conditioning, and presents an atmosphere of hustle.

It was pretty evident that you did what Coach Mannion wanted; you had to *earn* the right to play, or you rode the bench. There were no free rides on this team—everyone pulled their weight. I also saw that if a player made an honest mistake, he was immediately surrounded by his teammates, who made sure he felt a wave of positive support that helped him shake it off.

I leaned back on the bench, with the warm rays of the sun hitting my face, and admired Coach Mannion's attention to detail in drills, and his ability to run the show. I knew very quickly he was a seasoned educator and a born coach. His assistant coaches gave him the respect he deserved and listened to his every word, knowing that his many years of experience were earned. As the head coach, he was here to lead these young athletes and their new high school to victory. We all felt he was the right pick and a great addition to Mountainside High School. His football wisdom came from years of experience that included both winning and losing. His philosophy was ingrained into all his high school teams with hundreds of hours of practice, meetings, watching film, and playing games on Friday nights.

I was very pleased that my grandson had this man in his young life. Being a retired coach myself, I understood that Coach Mannion knew the secrets of winning. He'd won the high school state title at Silverton High School (in Silverton, Oregon) before coming to Mountainside. While sitting there watching practice, I had plenty of time to think back on my days as a coach and teacher, and how over the years I had gained wisdom and experience in coaching.

I watched this seasoned leader and smiled. This guy had my respect. He had earned this rite of passage and the right to make important football decisions. This leader had been in hundreds of situations and drew from his experiences. He knew what to do, and he knew what worked and what didn't.

It was easy for me, as a retired coach, sitting there on those hard metal bleachers, to appreciate the wisdom being demonstrated down on the field. I started thinking about the world today, and how we're trying to pass that wisdom on to a future generation. It seems in this fast-paced world, many people want to lead without having learned life's tough lessons first. Many people call themselves "leaders" after finding an early entry into a leadership role. They just want to make their mark and achieve recognition. But they are often unable to handle people and serious situations. They have a suitcase full of new ideas that may sound good but haven't been thought out. They tell people what they want to hear, while looking for instant credibility, attention, and fame.

These unseasoned leaders push their way into leadership and truly believe they have arrived. But they quickly get in over their heads and find out that they lack wisdom or experience to draw from. Over time, these kinds of leaders can keep us from doing things right. They cloud our vision, making us forget how we got here in the first place.

Smart leaders, on the other hand, have seen change. They welcome new ideas, but they have also seen many ideas come and go. They realize that making a change can be both rewarding and costly. Seasoned leaders know that too many changes too quickly can lead to confusion and a loss of direction and can bring about a negative result. Wisdom tells us we need to use common sense and pay attention to our leaders.

Change comes from good decisions made over time, to achieve good results.

Taking one last look at the field from high in the bleachers, I saw that practice was now coming to an end. It had been a good day. Down on the field, the team was starting to look pretty good, and we all knew why. Our head coach was a great leader. It seemed that wherever he went, the sun shone brightly.

In the years since, Coach Mannion's football program has evolved without too many changes to a football philosophy that has served him well. My grandson is in good hands! GO MAVERICKS!

P.S. The football season is over now, and the Mountainside Mavericks, with eight wins and four losses, made it to the playoffs. Not only that, but they knocked off the number one team in the state, the Tigard Tigers, 34–31, in an exciting overtime finish that will go down in Oregon high school history. Never has a number-sixteen-rated team knocked off a number-one-rated team in the history of Oregon high school football. As of now, the Mavericks have not won the state title, but there is always next year. Landon Sherman (number twelve) made third team all-metro and is looking forward to his next season as a Maverick with Coach Mannion at the helm. As a grandfather, I sit here very proud of my grandson and the team for going the distance, and Coach Mannion and his staff for their fine job this year!

COACHING PHILOSOPHIES

I think back on my experiences coaching and I'm so thankful that it was a part of my life. Coaching was good to me because I love to compete. I played football, baseball, and basketball for several years in junior high, high school, and college. I wasn't the biggest player on the field, so I hustled and played with a competitive edge.

By playing multiple sports, I acquired a sound feeling for the toughness and techniques needed to be competitive. I used my experiences as a player to inspire my teams as a coach. I wanted my teams to be tough competitors and well-prepared to play, but also to demonstrate good sportsmanship. They were always to play within the rules of the game. I pushed my teams toward smart, consistent offense, and aggressive, in-your-face defense.

In football, I witnessed many teams who lived and died (mostly the latter) by the pass. Their ability to block for the running game became average and their linemen lost the ability to stay with their blocks, and thus were unable to move the ball down the field consistently. I have always believed in running the football first and passing second. I felt running the ball produced the correct mindset for linemen when playing a tough opponent.

I tried to control a football game with sustained offensive drives to keep the football away from the opponent. You would be surprised how a good running game will wind down the clock and keep the football away from the other team. When they did get the ball, I would attack them aggressively on defense, using stunts. Over the years, I've seen football teams unable to generate a lot of offense. Sometimes they are held back by a defense that makes too many mistakes. I've seen coaches who didn't stick to their game plan. They made the mistake of not demanding accountability, and that sent the wrong message to their players. Instead of pushing players to get better at technique, they would get behind and go to the pass, never to recover.

Winning teams have great coaches, and great coaches develop great offensive and defensive players who love to perform under pressure. It's one of the secrets to winning. Confident players are the foundation of a team's success, and I believe the confidence of older players rubs off on the younger ones.

In basketball, I watch from the bleachers and see young teams play their first game, and it doesn't take long before their offense breaks down and they have trouble shooting the ball, or their defensive players are out of position and getting beat to the basket, or they're not putting pressure on the shooter. In baseball, I see young players come up to the plate forgetting to hit the ball *hard*. When infielders field a ground ball, I look for them to sit down and then gather themselves after the catch and come up smoothly to deliver a perfect throw. I'm always looking for fundamentals. To me, it's simple. It's all about working on fundamentals, over and over, and making players accountable.

Thoughts on Offense

Through my years as a coach, my offensive teams have been taught speed and deception. I know from experience that you need a certain amount of offense to play a game. Some coaches make the mistake of having too much offense, which confuses their players and creates inconsistent plays and bad timing.

When coaching young kids, I've always started with a few plays. Once you have decided which plays you're going to use, push your players to run those plays with speed, timing, and deception. Players need to be good actors. Remember, it's critical that your players feel comfortable running offense and defense. Whether you're coaching football, basketball, or baseball, you will need to be aggressive and quick. The secret is practicing and repeating drills until they become consistent. Your players will gain confidence and consistency as the season progresses.

Young players will need to spend extra time throwing the football, shooting the basketball, or hitting the baseball along with catching and throwing. As the weeks go by, the number of plays in your offensive playbook should increase conservatively, but your basic offensive plays should never change. Remember: your fundamentals are the heart of your offensive and defensive play, and coaches as well as players should be completely comfortable using them.

Over time, you will realize little things that help the offense and defense work—tricks of the trade, you might say. For example, flip-flopping the line or cutting down or opening your lineman splits in football. Going back door or using the give-and-go in basketball.

Hitting the ball hard in baseball. These simple fundamentals have been used to great success through the years by winning coaches.

Thoughts on Defense

Looking at defense I have felt most comfortable being very aggressive. A coach must know all the defensive positions and where players need to be at any time. As a head coach, knowing the defense will draw respect from your players as well as your assistant coaches. When you want or need to go to your defensive play, just call it out. For example, in football, you might hear the coach call out, "Base defense!" In basketball, you might hear the coach yell, "Man-to-man," or "Zone defense!" In baseball, aligning or positioning your players with hand signals during the game is important. All the coaches and players on the team should know exactly what needs to happen, where to line up, and what their assignments are. Having a simple way of communicating can help your team play more effectively.

Good Coaches

Good coaches understand and teach good techniques. This comes from many years of being a student of the game. I look for good assistant coaches who are not standing around talking about last week's fishing trip but are *coaching*. My feeling is that assistant coaches need to be coaching players—talking with them and helping them get better. There's a real art to being a good assistant coach, and I've always admired and respected those who help a program. Until you understand how to be a good assistant coach, it will be much harder to become a good head coach.

Being a coach at any level is a big responsibility. It requires many hours of discussion. You need to be able to draw plays, watch your team's performance, grade that performance, and communicate with other coaches and players. You also need to write good practice plans, scout opponents, and be there for long-distance car and bus rides. As a head coach, you will learn to speak to your players before a game. You must inspire them, explaining why giving one hundred percent for their team, school, parents, and community is so important and worth the effort. At the end of the game, you will need to talk to your team once again, whether they are full of cheers and shouts of victory, or the silence of being defeated. I can't tell you how many times I have been in both situations. To me, the athletic arena is a true classroom that teaches young people how to be strong in defeat and humble in victory while becoming great leaders.

The Easy and Tough Seasons

I like to think that I could have taken any group of players and had a winning season. I know the years that my teams were short on talent were tough. Not only did we not win games, but other parts of the program suffered. Coaches started questioning what we were doing and started looking for answers in the wrong places. Players started wondering if they could win a game. Parental support diminished, and you could feel the tension grow.

I learned very quickly that a team needs to have *some* talent or it's going to be a long season. It becomes a no-win situation. If the coach pushes the players to get better but the talent is not there, players can start having negative feelings about the program. On the other hand, if a team is winning games, the players continue to believe in their coaches and the program. I've found it's much easier for a team to get better if they're winning. I was fortunate to only have a few losing seasons in all my years of coaching.

Deciding to Play

When a student or parent asks my advice about playing, I try not to force or push their decision one way or another. With students, I ask a simple question: Do you think about playing, and wonder if you might like it? If the answer is yes, then I invite them to come to practice for a few days and try the sport out. If, after a few days, they aren't enjoying themselves, that's okay. I thank them for trying, and let them know that if they change their mind later, they will be welcome to try again. We never make them feel bad about trying something new.

If a player has already played the sport, or it's five weeks into the season and they want to stop, then our conversation is more serious. As coaches we don't want players to look back and feel like they quit for the wrong reason, or that they made a mistake. Parents normally prefer that their kids finish what they start, so we want to be sure that players, parents, and coaches are all on the same page when a player drops out. Sometimes, players will make the wrong decision and turn their gear in, only to regret it later.

Overweight players may find practices tough and want to turn in their gear. Carrying extra weight, given the constant running and demands of practice, can get them down. Good teams are aware of the extra effort needed by these players and support them in practice, cheering them on. I've seen players lose pounds by staying with it and then making huge gains in self-confidence that are reinforced by their peers. At the end of the season, we try to ensure they realize they have helped the team and gone the distance and are better for it.

Parents need to be careful when deciding whether to let a child play or not. My father almost didn't let me play, because, like most parents, he was afraid I would get hurt. But competing in sports utterly changed my life for the better and helped me develop as a young man. My coaches added to my life in so many positive ways. I would have hated to miss out on their influence. I *wanted* to play. Even now—fifty years later—I still love the games. And I still admire some of my coaches. I see them occasionally, to say hello.

Believing in Yourself and Your Team

Have you ever wondered why coaches have winning seasons? It's just like a great artist or a great singer. Whatever the craft, winners love what they do, and work hard to get the job done.

When I started coaching fifty years ago, I loved the game of football and wanted to become a great coach. I realized in college that I had the ability to teach others and help them achieve a higher level of performance. I then started obsessing over the different parts of a team and how they should function on the field.

When I became a middle-school teacher, I was given my first head coaching position. I remember talking with the players for the first time. I had just finished coaching little league baseball, and for two years we were undefeated. I wanted to achieve the same thing in football. I looked at my players sitting in the bleachers and introduced myself. I spoke for a moment and then took my new team to the parking lot to start running plays. Two weeks later, we won our first two games. And then, to my surprise, we lost the next five.

I'll never forget that first year. I realize now that learning twenty running plays and twenty passing plays was our downfall. I decided the following year to feature *eight* running plays and *eight* passing plays. I decided to keep it simple. After that, I never had another losing season.

I had learned a valuable lesson: KEEP IT SIMPLE!

LEARNING TO COACH FROM THE COACHES WHO INSPIRED ME

Through the years I have known and played for many great coaches. I remember them well, including their ability to develop young athletes. They all had unique personalities and the ability to create a winning atmosphere.

I'd like to share with you how I remember these special people, but before I do, I'll share a few lessons I learned over the years. As a new coach, fresh out of college, I learned very quickly that I needed to find my own style of doing things. Trying to coach like someone you once played for won't help you find your own way.

We all have watched experienced coaches and admired their abilities. They look comfortable running the show and being in charge. I don't think too many new coaches are immediately able to line up their players and then run the offense and defense with perfection. A lot of coaches start out coaching younger players and only later move to older ones. Most head coaches have been assistants before accepting the head coach job. They spent time observing their head coach, learning from his leadership of the team.

When starting as a head coach, find out what part of coaching you feel most comfortable with. Once you've determined your coaching strengths, find assistants who will complement your style. Fill the other coaching assignments where you need help. Draw from your other coaches' strengths and make sure they can support you on and off the field. Most head coaches bring at least one assistant coach who knows his program when changing coaching assignments.

Here are some coaches who impacted my own coaching career.

My first coach was E.G. Stassens, a very successful real estate broker in Beaverton, Oregon, in the 60s. I played for him in eighth grade. This was my first experience with tackle football. Coach Stassens was a great assessor of talent, and he was even better at teaching us how to run football plays. He was a perfectionist and understood the importance of deception and speed. Coach Stassens loved football and gave up his personal time for years to develop young players in our community. I was there because my P.E. teacher had told me that I was too rough for flag football; he thought I would hurt someone and that I should play tackle football instead.

Coach Stassens stood about 5'10" tall, and he had broad shoulders and short hair. He wore glasses and looked like a marine drill-sergeant. He did not mince words and was probably the fairest coach I ever played for. He treated all his players the same and never singled out another player in front of the team unless it was to say something positive. When he saw how aggressive I was, he wasted no time putting me at fullback, where I carried the football.

Coach Stassens explained to his players that their job was simply to run over the opposing team. We were to wear them down and then finish them off with play-action passes. He knew that using effective running plays between the tackles would open the outside run and enable us to use play-action passes. He also believed in conditioning his players, so we'd be in better shape than the other team and get less tired during games. His style was simple: control the game with the run and use up the clock. Our team that year had speed and size. I loved every minute of it, and it change my life. We were undefeated that year. Coach Stassens really made football fun and exciting, and I will never forget him.

My next coach was Darrel Mouse Davis, head coach at Sunset High School, also in Beaverton. Mouse helped to develop the run-and-shoot offense in high school, college, and the pros. He is remembered for his high-powered passing attack, setting attendance records, and points scored throughout the United States and Canada. Mouse has become a football legend and has been inducted into the Oregon Sports Hall of Fame and Museum.

I played for Coach Davis for three years in high school. He was without a doubt one of the most dynamic people I ever met. Mouse was rock solid on what he wanted from his offense. Once again, I played fullback for his team, and I made sure the defensive end never got to the quarterback. On rainy and windy nights, when the passing was tough, Mouse would call on his running attack to control the game by running his fullback up the middle, then hitting them with the counter-play, and finally optioning to the outside with sweeps and reverses.

Coach Davis could look straight through you in practice and then afterward show a wonderful sense of humor. He cared for and respected his players. I can still remember the Wednesday practices fifty years later. I'd wonder if I'd get through the conditioning and still be able to walk! Mouse had a legendary ability to fire up his team. He created an atmosphere for winning. His personality was one-of-a-kind. He was born to be head coach. Mouse stood about 5'6". He'd played quarterback in college with poise, speed, and deception. He had a dynamic ability to lead his teams. Once again, I will never forget Coach Darrel Mouse Davis.

The last coach I will share with you is Ad Rutschman, who was one of the finest high school and college coaches in the country. During his career, he won numerous baseball and football league titles while coaching at Hillsboro High School, in Hillsboro, Oregon. After winning state championships in both sports at Hillsboro, he accepted the head football and baseball coach position at Linfield University (known as Linfield College at the time).

In just a few years, Coach Rutschman won his first national baseball championship and then claimed two national football championships. He was inducted into both the Oregon Sports Hall of Fame and Museum and the College Football Hall of Fame. I played against Coach Rutschman in high school, and then, after serving in Vietnam, I came home and played for him in college. He was outstanding at developing successful players. While at Linfield, Coach Rutschman built a football and baseball dynasty. Even today, the streak continues in football, with sixty-nine winning seasons. That's the most continuous winning seasons of any college in the country!

Ad Rutschman's teams were always fine-tuned and ready to compete. One of his secrets was finding the other team's weaknesses and exploiting them. Coach Rutschman also possessed an unbelievable amount of energy and stamina. Back in the day, he was known as the "Flying Dutchman." Even today, his legacy continues. His grandson, Adly Rutschman, is already known for his toughness and ability to bring home the blue ribbon as a professional baseball player.

I will always remember the Rutschman family at Linfield. I will always be grateful for the chance to play for such a fine coach, and in such a wonderful program. I will not forget Joan "Mama Cat" Rutschman, Ad Rutschman's wife. She was wonderful and respected by all, and she was a special part of Coach Rutschman's career and life.

These three coaches were the best of the best, and they earned their success with hard work and dedication.

COACHING TECHNIQUES

Teaching good technique is vital to having your players understand the game and perform at a high level.

When I started coaching, I made the mistake of talking too much during drills. I thought explaining every detail to a player would help him get better. It did help, but it also took time away from practice. I learned over the years to simplify what I wanted by using short one- or two-word comments and moving on to the next player. That, plus repetition, was the real secret to improving a player's technique.

I talk about my one-liners in the next section of this book, showing how players would communicate during a baseball game, for instance, to be ready for defensive situations. I believe in simplifying everything as much as you can and then practicing over and over so players automatically know what to do. If I owned a business, I would do the same thing, so my employees felt comfortable with the techniques needed in their jobs.

When you first start teaching a new technique, it's not going to be pretty. But after the players get the general idea and perform the technique over and over, you will be amazed at how they improve. Scientific proof backs this up. Individuals learn faster with short two- or three-word comments, rather than long explanations. In an athletic competition, there's no time for long explanations, so coaches usually yell out one-liners. Once the players have the techniques down, then you can add accountability and competition.

There is no shortcut to victory!

COACHING ONE-LINERS

I'd like to explain one-liners and my reasons for using them. If you spend time watching young athletic teams, you'll notice that many of them haven't learned how to communicate during a game. Many players don't realize that talking to their fellow players can prepare the team for the next situation, making them a little more alert. When teams don't talk, they're missing out on opportunities to make more plays. Communication helps each other understand what's going on in each moment.

For example, in baseball, here are some of the one-liners you might hear from more experienced players. If you're up to bat, players might say, "Hit the ball hard," "Choke up," "Tag on a fly ball," "Lay off the high ones." If you're playing defense, communication might sound like this: "No soft throws," "Get the first one," "Chest-high throws," "Sit on a ground ball," "Get rid of the ball," and others.

In football, one-liners might sound like this: "On defense," "Get to the quarterback," "Square up on the tackle," "Watch your containment lanes," "Strip the football," "Create a fumble," "Hands up on a pass." On offense, you might hear these: "Seven count block," "Good handoffs," "Catch the football," "Linemen get off the ball," "No fumbles," and "Quiet in the huddle."

These short one-liners teach players how to communicate and remember important points in both practice and games.

Each season I was coaching, I had only a short period to get the team ready for their first game. It was coaching on the run. I didn't have time in practice to stop and talk for ten or twenty minutes on how and why I wanted things a certain way. I did more talking later in the season, but at the start we were in a rush. During drills, I would shout out one-liners, verbalizing to the players how to play and what to think about in different situations. I pushed them and held them accountable by calling out the one-liners. I knew I had done a good job when the players talked it up during games, using the same one-liners they'd learned in practice.

One-liners can disrupt the other team's play, talking them out of what they wanted to call because they think you're already prepared for it. I believe in my one-liners; there's no question they helped us play better and smarter. The more players call out one-liners, the more effective they become. It doesn't matter what the sport is—using one-liners helps teach your kids to communicate and be ready.

NO SHORTCUTS TO VICTORY!

It's not easy to build a winning program, no matter what sport you're coaching. As a head coach, you want to make good decisions at the right time without taking any shortcuts. Building a successful athletic program demands experienced, strong leadership and a clear vision for winning. Head coaches need to have the ability and confidence to sell their ideas, drawing from their past experiences. They know building a good team requires a good staff to help carry the load. Developing lasting relationships with your assistant coaches, players, and community is one of the keys to winning.

Most head coaches are respected and bring with them knowledge of the sport, positive energy, and enthusiasm. They remain positive and driven throughout the season. They show appreciation to players when winning, but also demonstrate optimism after suffering a loss.

There's no doubt the head coach's job is tough. Having a winning philosophy and direction for the program takes a special leader. The coaching staff must work hard to instill confidence, dedication, and hard work in everyone, so the team has a chance to win. This means pushing everyone involved and asking for many hours of their time so the team can negotiate numerous challenges and difficulties along the way. Winning takes everyone doing their part for their teammates and the program. There are no shortcuts to victory. The feeling must be *all for one and one for all*. Players must depend on each other to become winners. They will learn to see, feel, and practice what makes each other perform at a higher level. It's all part of a growing process.

Growth takes time and hard work. Head coaches and assistant coaches must hold players accountable for improving and delivering a good performance on and off the field. When players do well, great coaches show appreciation. They are excited for the players' success and let them know they've done a good job. Good programs make a point of building players' confidence, lifting the morale of everyone. When players deliver a solid performance and the team wins, the community becomes excited and jumps on board. That support in turn helps the team win later games. It all carries over to the team's ability to play well and have a great experience. Coaches, players, and parents want to feel good about their team. When they do, they treat each other with more respect, and they share how proud and excited they are to be a part of the winning feeling. On the other hand, if the team performs poorly and shows poor character, morale heads in a downward spiral, and all who are connected to the program feel less excited about what the team can achieve. The community becomes less supportive, and relationships become strained.

To have a good program, coaches must be sharp and have positive attitudes, while making positive adjustments that are directed toward getting better. These adjustments need to be well thought out and implemented at the right time. For example, installing a new offense on a football team is a serious decision. It can be beneficial or a serious mistake. Your reason for the change needs to be very well thought out. If your team is winning, then you might want to leave the offense alone and not mess with what's working. Move slower on the changes when you're winning. If you're losing, then maybe it's time to try a new direction. You don't see many winning teams installing a new offense halfway through the season.

My belief is that all teams need a certain amount of talent to win. Teams low on talent need coaches who can be creative and continue to build, motivate, and deliver a positive experience. Great coaches motivate players to play better, work harder, and grow. They bring out their team's best on the field.

WINNING AND LOSING

Winning and losing can be a two-edged sword. Everyone wants to win and have the feeling of being good at what they do. Winning makes getting ready for the next game a little easier. With each win, players build confidence and faith in themselves and their team. Fans' support makes winning even more enjoyable because of the positive feedback and excitement. Everyone feels good about being part of a winner.

The problem with winning is that it can lead to overconfidence. A team can lose focus and the capacity to play hard. It's not easy keeping players motivated and prepared to play week after week at a level needed to win. Some teams have such great players that the wins come easy. Other teams may play in a weak league or conference and then develop an unrealistic confidence in their ability to win.

As a coach, I would rather play close games, so my players face real competition. I have found that easy wins aren't good ways to build strong character. They give a false sense of how good you really are. Most teams improve week by week, and if your schedule is too easy, it can be a real eye-opening experience to play a tough opponent.

Coaches can do things to help keep players competitive. Having competitive drills in practice where players must perform and be held accountable against their own teammates is just one idea. Making sure they remain in shape physically and ready to compete can also help. Motivational talks can inspire players to believe in each other and set goals to play their best. Finally, players should be taught to study the next opponent and be prepared to win.

Losing is not much fun to talk about. I hate getting up on a Saturday morning and having to look myself in the mirror while thinking of a loss suffered the night before. I hate losing! But it's important talk about it, so let's do that.

Chances are, you're not going to win every contest. I used to think winning every game was great for players and that it promoted success. But now that I'm older and wiser I can see that losing one or even two games can also teach us some good lessons. Specifically, we learn that life goes on, and that at 3:30 p.m. on Monday, we'll start all over again, and have just four days to be ready for the next game.

When you lose, the people around you watch to see how you handle it. And how you should handle it is simple: start all over on Monday by looking at what went wrong with the last game and fixing it. Coaches should let their players know that each game is a challenge; what matters is how we move forward and get better. If we work hard and teach our players to play with great character, then we can be proud of how we played, whether we win or lose.

Every team gets knocked down sometimes. It's what you do *after* you get beat that others will watch. Put a bad game behind you and learn from it. Let it go, look ahead to your next opponent, and commit to playing better.

VICTORY WITH CLASS!

We've all participated in athletic contests in which there have been heated discussions and even confrontations between players, coaches, and referees. After a contested game, spectators walk away shaking their heads and talking about the injustices, and how the other team got lucky because the referees missed a call that cost them the game.

After playing and coaching for years, I realize calls and penalties are going to be missed. Professional coaches and seasoned players understand that it's part of the game and learn to walk away with class. During the game, when coaches talk to the referees about a situation, they try to explain their side of the story with respect. After all, it's not easy being a referee, and even the best ones can't make perfect calls every time.

Coaches who ride the referees—treating them disrespectfully—find out the hard way that it reflects on their team. Referees are human. They will listen to only so much negative feedback before taking appropriate action. If spectators witness their coach getting after a referee, they might think it's okay to start making similar comments from the stands, which can bring about even more negativity. I've always respected the coaches who have a professional demeanor on and off the field. I believe that it carries over to the players.

Remember: victory with class! (I wish I could say I was perfect in this regard, but that would not be true.)

IF IT'S WORKING, DON'T MESS WITH IT

I was once watching University of Oregon head coach Chip Kelly on television and announced to all who were watching with me that this would be his last year at Oregon. They all looked at me and commented how wrong I was. But that coach ended up leaving the next year.

On TV, Kelly looked different. He lacked energy standing there on the sidelines. I thought he was ready for something new. I could see it in his body language. As head coach for the previous few seasons, he had helped create a new style of football, and it changed everything. His teams were winning big. I think he loved the development process, and after receiving a lot of attention for creating a winning philosophy, he wanted something bigger, and started looking for a new challenge.

Over the course of a few years, we'd watch him, witnessing his great coaching abilities. He and his coaching staff created an atmosphere of great hustle and great performance. His coaching style demanded other teams defend against a sped-up style of football. With this sped-up offense and time-management philosophy, his teams excelled. Everyone—and I mean everyone—watched in amazement at how the Oregon Ducks performed. Other coaches changed their game plans, trying to figure out how to slow down the Oregon team. This new style of football drew some of the best athletes in the country to play at Oregon. The team had it all and couldn't be stopped. It just got better and better.

But when Coach Kelly decided to leave, this new winning style of football went with him, and the big victories were over. The Ducks tried to hold on to the philosophy, but the new coach didn't have the same vision. The football program changed, and the belief was gone.

My point is this: the head coach needs to have the confidence and the ability to put the pieces together and create a winning program. If you have a great coaching staff and your teams are winning, keep it going—hold on to that combination. With every coaching change, you risk undoing what's already working.

Now that some years have passed, a new group of coaches have emerged at Oregon, with a new, solid brand of football. Once again, the Oregon teams are winning. Hopefully, this successful combination of talent and coaches will be there for some time to come.

PREPARING TO WIN

Preparing to win takes time and hard work. You need to know everything about your opponent.

If you can watch them compete, so much the better. Learn your opponent's tendencies from past competitions. Study their strengths and weaknesses, and never take them for granted. I can't tell you how many nights I've spent trying to eliminate problems that might hurt our efforts to beat an opponent. I also spent time figuring out ways to exploit opponents' weaknesses to gain the advantage.

Coaches and players spend many hours preparing for a competition. One method is to watch opponents on a big screen television as a team and recognize their tendencies. This helps a team recognize and react quicker to different situations. Nowadays, players can also study opponents at home, watching them compete on YouTube and elsewhere on the internet. In practice, players use what they've learned to achieve a competitive edge. When it's time to compete, both opponents know each other and have a good idea how to win.

COACHING PLAYERS

Occasionally, I've seen a coach yell at a player in front of the rest of the team. I don't believe this type of coaching benefits the program or the players. It destroys players' confidence and hurts team morale.

In my own coaching, however, I'd light a fire under the team's butt to get them to practice harder! I also believe bad language on the field by players and coaches is not acceptable. It brings down morale and makes the program less classy. Great coaches put the player first. My reason for coaching was always to help young people grow positively. I refused to jeopardize a student athlete's well-being to win a football game.

I would, however, push my athletes to a level of performance that we coaches thought they were capable of. Players need to know that coaches care about them and their well-being. I've never met a player who *wants* to fail. They all have different reasons for being on the field. I've seen a first-time player in his first football game pick off a pass and run sixty yards down the field to score his first touchdown. It changed his whole life.

Sadly, I have also seen a player crushed by what a coach said— made to feel bad about himself, his confidence taken away. As a coach, I will always try to bring out the best in a player and give him an opportunity to have a great moment.

MENTORING YOUR PLAYERS

I've always tried to send a message to my players that I will do everything I can to give them a great moment in football.

A coach's relationship with his players can help build positive atmosphere around the team. Players want to know the coaching staff cares about them and sees them as a valuable part of the team. As a coach, I try to help players any way I can, in a professional manner, on and off the field. I've always tried to inspire my players to give one hundred percent, so that, win or lose they can be proud of their effort. Winning and losing is not just about the scoreboard. It's about learning to work hard, perform consistently, and be a good example for the community.

We coaches spend time talking about citizenship to inspire our players to become winners in their daily lives. What we're looking for in our players is to do the right thing daily. When a recruiter calls and wants to know about a player, their first question is not about football. Instead, they ask what else he brings to the team *besides* points on the scoreboard. Is he doing the right thing consistently, every day?

During football season there are going to be problems that players need help with, including injuries, relationships, time management, academics, and so on. Coaches are there to help them solve these problems and direct them professionally. If a player knows that his coach cares about him and wants him to have a great experience on the team, there's no question the player will perform better and more consistently.

EVALUATING PLAYERS

Evaluating your players is essential to winning and determining your team's strengths and weaknesses. It helps coaches determine what's working and what's not. The resulting information is useful to coordinate practices and prepare individuals and teams for competition. Coaches spend hours watching players compete to evaluate their strengths and weaknesses, helping them play more effectively.

Evaluating a team is an ongoing process, and the information collected needs to be studied to bring about the best decisions for winning. Scouts and coaches attend athletic events to evaluate future athletes and show their interest. They watch and study players' performances and start building relationships early. That way, if an athlete becomes part of their program, the transition is smooth, and the new player quickly feels valued and part of the team.

No one really knows where these new players will end up in the scheme of things. Especially in high school sports, I've witnessed small, weak athletes getting knocked around by bigger, stronger players, but then grow into their bodies and become major assets to the team. They continue to excel, and before you know it, you're looking at a college All-American.

Don't ever count anyone out! We've all heard the story of Michael Jordan, one of the best professional basketball players ever. He was cut from the varsity basketball team in high school and ended up becoming a superstar in the NBA. Albert Einstein was not a great student, but he went on to become one the world's most gifted mathematicians. The point is, you never know what level of performance someone will achieve. Watching them grow is important to your winning program.

Here is what I look for in an athlete: talent, citizenship, coaching ability, being a quick learner, hustle, drive, respect, a strong work ethic, leadership ability, good grades, goals, family support, neatness, confidence, and swagger. And this is just a partial list! If an athlete has talent and needs help getting better, I will always try to help, as an educator first and a coach second. Remember, there is no shortcut to victory!

BIGGER STRONGER AND FASTER

Getting ready to compete takes time. Time to prepare physically, mentally, and emotionally.

I'd like to share my story of being a young athlete and getting ready to play college football, and how hard it was to get my chance to play. Playing college football was one of the greatest experiences of my life, but it wasn't easy getting there. My first attempt didn't last long. One day, a couple of high school teammates asked me to visit with the football coach from Columbia Basin Junior College, in Pasco, Washington. After a short interview, their offer sounded pretty good. I packed my bags and headed to Pasco to try out for the Columbia Basin Hawks. I had no plan, nor had I prepared for this attempt to play in college, but it sounded good, and I wanted to try.

I thought I would play for two years at Columbia Basin and then transfer to Eastern Washington University and play two years there, getting my four-year degree. When I arrived at tryouts, I worked hard to become the starting nose guard. I played five games for the Hawks and was being written up as a first-year junior college All-American. I was playing well but doing terrible in the classroom. Even though the newspapers were saying good things about me on the field, I was having a hard time.

I hadn't planned or prepared for this adventure, and that uncertainty started to take its toll. First, I didn't have enough money for food. My football scholarship only paid for tuition and books. Plus, I was living in the basement of an old house, which was dark, cold, and damp. At that time, I had little interest in studying, and my grades were in the toilet. It wasn't long before I was exhausted, and I became sick with mononucleosis. After seeing a doctor, I was told that I needed complete rest. With that, my football season was over. My dream of being a first-year All American went out the window.

I realized I needed to go back home and heal, so I dropped out of school. That was the end of my first attempt to play college football. Next, I joined the military and spent two years serving in Vietnam. During my military service, I had plenty of time to think about returning to the gridiron, and how, this time, I would be ready. When I came home, I was focused and determined to try again. A few weeks after returning, I enrolled at Portland Community College in Portland, Oregon. I attended classes for two terms and spent time learning to study. I passed my classes, brought my grades up, and applied to Linfield University (at the time, it was called Linfield College), in McMinnville, Oregon. After talking with the head football coach, I was granted permission to walk on, and given a chance to make the team and earn a three-year educational grant. The educational grant would pay for my classes, books, meals, and a small room in one of the dorms.

Linfield was a classy program. Participating would be a great challenge, but I had come a long way for this second chance, and I wasn't going to be denied. Though it was never easy, I was determined. I made the team but had to redshirt my first year after breaking my collarbone in practice. I came back the next year and started for the Wildcats for the next two seasons. I was only 5'8" tall, and I weighed 195 pounds. I was by far the smallest defensive lineman in the league.

During the summers while attending Linfield, I worked at a private health club, using it to my advantage. I watched and learned from other athletes while working out. One of the important lessons I learned was that I needed to get bigger, stronger, and faster. I also found out that many competitive athletes stay in shape all year round, depending on their sport. Others—for example, football players—stay in shape for a much shorter period.

Being a football player, I felt twelve weeks would be enough time to get ready for the first practice. After a long, hard season of football, players who have had lots of contact or been injured need to rest their bodies so they can heal. During the off season they still spend time working out, but in a more relaxed way.

During those three years playing for Linfield, I pushed myself hard from June until late August to be in shape and ready to compete. I worked hard every day, getting bigger, stronger, and faster. Fortunately, working at a health club in the summers gave me complete access to the weight room, pool, and the motivation of other people who were pushing themselves also.

My weeks looked like this. On Monday, I would start out doing a circuit with the free weights. On Tuesday, I would be on the weight machines. Then I would go back and forth every other day and switch from free weights to weight machines. I spent time each day in the pool, swimming laps and pushing off the side of the pool with my legs for quicker starts. After the pool, I would lay down on one of the lounge chairs and take a forty-five-minute nap.

What a great way to spend the summer and get ready to play. I make it sound easy, but it wasn't—lifting weights especially was hard work. But I loved every minute, and I pushed myself. I had something to prove: I wanted to be an All-American. In the evenings, I continued my workout at the local high school. I started by running 240-yard sprints from goal post to goal post. My goal was for each sprint to be under 35 seconds. When I first ran sprints, I could run maybe five sprints under time. At the end of the summer, I could run twenty-five, each under 35 seconds. There was little doubt I was ready for my first practice.

As I ran my sprints, my endurance and speed improved. This helped me physically and mentally. My speed and endurance were strong. I felt like I could run forever. On Tuesday and Thursday workouts, I would practice 40-yard sprints and 10-yard shuttle runs, all timed with a stopwatch. I became very quick and very strong!

The summer evenings were hot, and at the end of the day I would relax by sitting out on the deck with my father, talking about playing and getting ready. He was my support, and he believed in me. Some nights, I would put on a tank top and shorts and go for a five-mile run. I kid you not—by the end of the summer, I could run until the sun came up. Remember the movie *Rocky*, and how weak he started out, and how strong he became? That's the feeling you get when you're in shape.

Remember, there's no shortcut to victory. That's how you get to playing at a higher level—and every player who shows up for college football is good. Between lifting weights and running, I knew I had worked hard to be ready, and I was.

My workouts with the weights went something like this. I would start out with 100 sit-ups and 100 push-ups. I would then move on to the leg extension machine and then do toe raises with weight on my shoulders. The toe raises were one of my secrets to becoming quicker; they helped me explode off the line of scrimmage. The bench press was next; I lifted 250 pounds, doing 10 reps. Then it was on to the squat machine. Rather than lifting a lot of weight and doing just one squat, I would use less weight and do 10 reps for endurance. The bench press gave me upper-body strength to neutralize the offensive linemen's charge. The squats helped me lift with my back and meet the oncoming blockers, so I could shed them and pursue the ball carrier. When I was at my peak, I was curling 200 pounds and had 16" biceps and triceps that helped deliver hard shots to opposing players.

I won't go over the complete workout, but I was very strong physically and mentally. Lifting weights had a lot to do with my mental and physical toughness. The stronger I got, the tougher I was. It gave me a feeling of confidence and determination. It took many hours of hard work to achieve that level of competitiveness. I wasn't the biggest player, so I played with an attitude. Like I said, I had something to prove. I was strong, fast, and determined to win!

WHAT'S FAITH GOT TO DO WITH IT?

This is not an easy topic to discuss, for fear of offending someone else's idea of faith when competing in athletics. These thoughts are mine and mine alone. This is about how faith helps athletes compete at a higher level and keeps them grounded through good and bad times.

A great example of an athlete's faith can be seen in the quarterback who played for the Seattle Seahawks, Russell Wilson. After leaving Seattle, he went through some tough times on the field playing for Denver, and his quarterback play was questionable. This continued while he was there (as of this writing, Russell plays for the Pittsburgh Steelers).

My feelings and ideas about what happened to Russell in Denver are very simple. Russell simply never felt at home with the fans and coaching staff in Denver. The Denver fans were fickle about showing support for Russell's ability. I saw it in his face when he was standing on the sidelines. He just didn't feel a real connection.

Even though Russell was going through hard times he continued to rely on his faith to turn things around. From where I sat, I saw that Russell's faith was not enough—he needed the care and support of the Denver fans to play at the top of his game. The people of Denver didn't realize how important they were to Russell's success. They just didn't get it—they were trying to take a shortcut to victory, and it wasn't working. They were missing the whole point, which was that Russell needed to feel that the fans believed.

I wanted to say, "Wake up, Denver! Believe in your quarterback and let him know you have his back." Russell has always played for something greater than himself, which allows him to play with great determination and confidence. Russell gets his "go juice" from the fans and all those around him.

Faith like Russell's has worked for many athletes over time. It has helped athletes play for the right reasons and helped them perform at a higher level. It has freed them to not worry about how many touchdowns are scored or how many passes are completed. It has allowed them to play their best football without getting down on themselves. Faith and support simply allow athletes to have confidence, whether winning or losing. That confidence elevates leadership during games and helps build long-lasting relationships with fans, other players, and coaches. It helps athletes play with swagger and moxie, which a quarterback especially needs to win.

Faith brings about exciting moments on the field, inspiring fans to celebrate their team. Denver fans needed to *believe* in Russell and then sit back and watch him play. Unfortunately, their support when he arrived was short-lived, and they were judgmental. Until Denver understands that there are no shortcuts to victory, and until they truly support their players, the Super Bowl is out of reach and just a dream.

For me, there is nothing bad about players having faith in

themselves and letting that faith guide them to be a more exciting athlete. Remember, when a player makes a great play and then points upward to the heavens, he's just celebrating by saying thank you! Faith is the complete trust in someone or something. The Seattle fans (also known as team's "the twelfth man") gave Russell Wilson the complete trust he needed to perform well. The more trust and support Russell got, the better he played, and the more games he won. Seattle's new quarterback is getting better each week, because in Seattle the fans have faith.

Tell me this—how many of you ever question Tom Brady's ability? I know I never did. Everyone believes in Tom Brady and Peyton Manning. They received the support they needed to win. True support is trusting your players to get the job done, and Tom Brady and Peyton Manning both felt that from the fans. It added confidence and moxie to their play—a confidence and moxie never seen in quarterbacks.

Fans need to learn how to believe and have faith. I'll take Russell Wilson anytime because I have faith that he will find a way to win! I simply like who he is as a person.

"MAN OF THE YEAR"? RIGHT!

I was watching a video a few days ago and witnessed a player arrogantly put himself above other players. This display was in front of thousands of watching fans. It has bothered me ever since.

It wasn't the first time I'd observed this behavior from this individual. As a coach and classroom teacher for over 40 years, seeing it made my blood boil. His treatment of others told me everything I needed to know about him. A few minutes later, the announcers indicated he was up for man of the year award for helping kids. Yeah, right!

Over the years, I've coached similar players. Their success is always short-lived. Sure, I've wanted my players to play with confidence and even a little swagger. But I also want them to remain humble and not too cocky. It's not just athletes who get too big for their britches, of course. In all walks of life, we find people who become successful and then think that everyone should venerate them. In contrast, sometimes we see the true Samaritan, who is thankful for their successes; these are just plain good people with good character. People like this are the real deal. They're not only good at what they do. They are thankful for the help they received and their chance to be where they are.

Remember: competing in sports, like any other competition, is simply participation in an extended classroom—a chance to become not only a skilled competitor, but a better human being.

TEAM LEADERSHIP

Every year you can hear the start of the new sports season, as athletes compete and fans cheer their teams on. Every so often, a ball flies over the fence, or there is a great catch in the end zone for six points, and the fans will go crazy with excitement. Hot dogs will be cooking on the grill, and popcorn and snow cones will be handed out. Parents will sit in the stands and visit, talking about their sons and daughters.

Yes, it's time to play once again, and the sun is out, bringing warmth to the fans excited to see players compete. As we listen to the sounds of teams cheering, and coaches pushing their players to be their very best, we realize these are some of the best moments we will ever experience.

Every year brings a new group of players, who are asked to pass on the torch for a winning season. They are also asked to practice toughness, perfection, brotherhood, and mutual respect. Returning players are given the responsibility of setting the tone for new players. At the end of the first practice, players come together and talk about what's expected, and the effort needed to achieve success.

As a coach, I believe that you can only become a leader and a stronger person when you are part of a team. It's a time for players to walk the talk and set the right example in handling tough situations on the field. They've been taught to play with respect for other players, coaches, umpires, and referees, while learning to be fierce competitors. Parents look to our coaches to watch over the team, making sure the game is a positive experience for everyone in the community. Coaches realize that teaching responsibility to young people can be very powerful and beneficial, providing the opportunity for them to grow. This is shown with each passing week as teams rise to the occasion with outstanding performances and new levels of success and confidence.

Week after week, players work hard in practice, getting ready to compete in the next game. On game day, win or lose, players set the tone. They are competing to win, and they will not give up. When a team is victorious, it's the coach's job to teach players to be humble in victory and show respect for the losing team. And if the coach's team is the losing team, players should be taught to hold their heads up and show good sportsmanship.

Competing in sports and being on a team is a great classroom for young people to grow strong, confident, and well-prepared for the future.

I right 23 counter

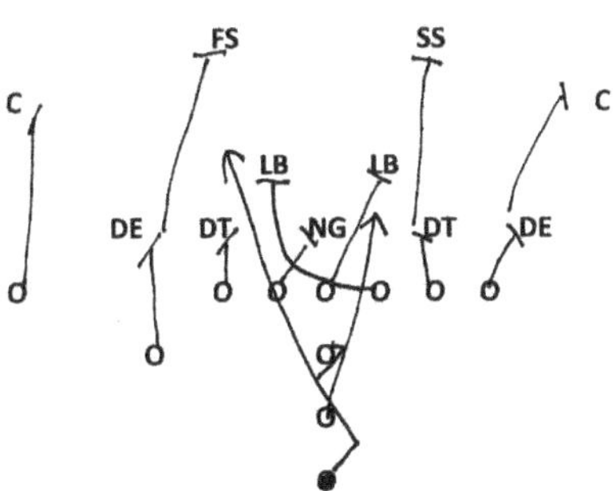

REPETITION

Repetition is one of the true secrets to becoming good at your craft. Through many hours of repetition, you become aware of and sensitive to the small important details that set you apart from others. You learn to feel, smell, touch, hear, and see the secrets necessary to becoming better.

During hundreds of hours of competition, you will experience many victories and some defeats. Celebrate the victories and hold them close—they will give you confidence to move forward. Learn from the defeats and remember what you learned. Don't dwell on the losses. Let them pass. Don't look back, but rather continue your journey. Remember: defeats are part of the path to greatness.

At times, you might need to step back and take a break, reflecting on where you've been and where you're headed. Even during a break, without knowing it, you will still be growing, processing the secrets you have learned. The truly good players and coaches learn from seasoned veterans who over the years have acquired wisdom and skill, through repetition and time.

ACCOUNTABILITY AND PRACTICE TEMPO

The rewards of practice are lost without accountability and tempo. For both individual players and the team, improvement depends on what type of atmosphere you develop in practice.

Most sports are played in a time-sensitive and competitive environment. Practicing at a slow, noncompetitive pace, and not insisting that your players perform, is the road to mediocrity. Practicing at a fast tempo sets the stage for your players to be in better physical shape, make better decisions, make more plays, and win more games.

If your team isn't working hard in practice, then it's your job as coach to light a fire under their butt and give them a reason to try harder. It's more important that players respect coaches first and like them second. Accountability and practice tempo are two secrets to success on the athletic field. Even with talented players, laziness in practice leads to inconsistency, average play, and a lack of success under pressure.

ATTITUDE!

During my college days, I played football and baseball for the Linfield Wildcats in McMinnville, Oregon. Linfield University, which was called Linfield College back then, was known for its great baseball and football teams. Today it remains a respected program.

The only difference between today and when I played is that the Wildcats have since won three national baseball titles and three national football titles. They also have the record for the longest number of consecutive winning football seasons of any college in the nation. Sixty-nine years without a losing football season—that's not bad!

As a young athlete, I witnessed this great program being born and was privileged to take part in it. The coaches were professional, and they cared for and respected their players. At that time, my playing philosophy was very simple. Do what it takes to get the job done, do it right, and do it with a smile. That's what I tried to model every day as a Wildcat.

One day, while I was on the field, the coach started talking with me. He complimented me on how hard I worked and my great attitude in practice. He told me what a good player I was becoming and how he appreciated my approach and my willingness to work hard. When he was done, I said thanks, and told him it was great to be a Wildcat.

My point in telling this story is to show how worthwhile it was to do whatever it took to earn my coach's respect. His praise for a job well done always lifted me up. I remembered that conversation and used the same approach when I started coaching. I lifted my players up and gave them confidence to get the job done. They loved to hear me call out their names and simply say, "GREAT JOB!"

I'm retired now, and I can look back at my efforts in the different jobs I've had. Some jobs, I admit, were not my favorite. But my approach never changed. Then and now, my can-do approach to work and coaching formed a solid foundation for success. In those years, I received a lot of respect and benefitted from doing my best and working hard. If I made a mistake, I apologized, and promised not to let it happen again.

In my coaching, having a positive approach always paid off. My players played better because of it. There's no question that I was demanding and tough during games, and on the practice field. But I made sure the kids also saw me smile, so they knew I loved them and the game. To me, having a positive attitude has been one of the most important ways I achieved success.

Not giving up, working hard, doing what's right, and building a positive atmosphere of respect, on and off the field—these are solid lessons to being a good coach.

INJURIES

Injuries are an inevitable part of high-level athletic competition, especially when it comes to contact sports. Athletes should report serious injuries to their head coach. Coaches need to have peace of mind that players are able to compete safely and that they are protected from additional injuries.

As a coach, I always tried to evaluate my players' injuries as soon as possible. During a game, we tried to have a team doctor on the bench, or at least nearby. Athletic teams should make a point of having a medical professional nearby during every contest. Most sports programs require an injured player to obtain a signed doctor's release and written permission from parents before returning to the game. Before a season begins, players are given physicals to screen for problems, and to ensure they are healthy enough to play. Physicals will reveal any additional problems players might have—for example, allergies to bee stings, asthma, and other problems that could be serious. Coaches need to carry a copy of the players' permission forms, insurance information, and emergency contact information with the team during practice and games, as well as while transporting players to and from competitions.

Remember: there's no shortcut to victory!

TRAINING RULES

Training rules are necessary for keeping athletes responsible for their actions during the season. When athletes compete in sports programs, they represent their communities and must be held accountable. Guidelines for eligibility and competition must be well thought out and enforced by serious consequences.

During the different sports seasons, coaches should be clear on the rules for competing in each sport. To help, sports programs often offer "parents' night" at the start of a season. Parents are asked to attend and meet with coaches to go over individual team rules, as well as school-district eligibility guidelines. Those guidelines might stipulate that an athlete needs to be passing five out of seven classes and have at least a 2.0 grade-point average to compete. Or they might establish consequences for substance abuse: if a player is found drinking or using drugs, for instance, his first offense could be suspension from playing in two games, as well as attending counseling and weekly drug screening for a time. After a second offense, the athlete might be automatically removed from the team and prohibited from participating in school activities for the rest of the semester.

These are just examples. Team rules are different for each sport and administered by the head coach after being cleared by the school administration. At parents' night, the athletes and parents are asked to sign a contract stating that they understand the district rules and the individual team rules. If an athlete breaks any of the rules, his parents are notified, and a meeting is set up to decide if he needs to be disciplined.

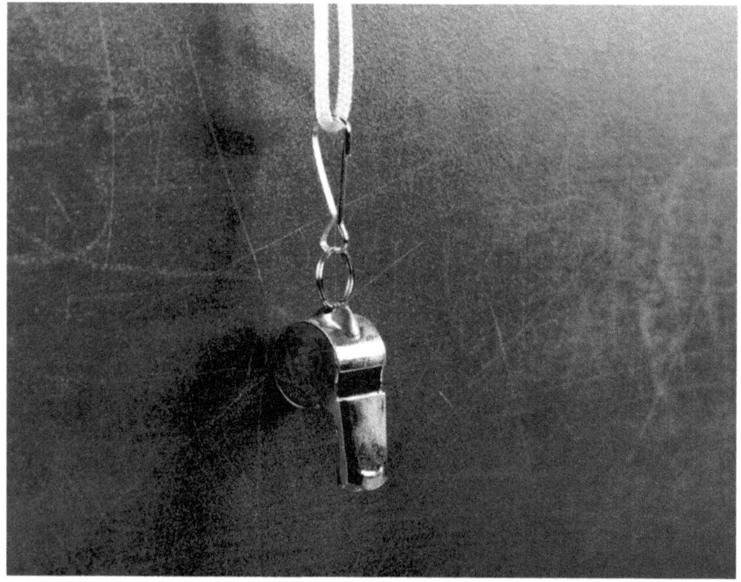

TEAM MANAGEMENT

Team management on and off the field is one of the keys to having a great athletic program. How your team acts in the locker room is just as important as their performance on the field.

Most teams show great class when competing and representing their community away from home. Sadly, we've all witnessed teams who do the opposite, earning the title of being jerks. Other important areas of team management include sportsmanship on and off the field, student behavior in the classroom and around school, and hustling during practice and competition. The purpose of team management is to teach citizenship and build a sound foundation for your sports program.

SPORTSMANSHIP ON THE SIDELINES

An athletic competition can get intense and exciting. It's easy to take out your frustrations on the officials if you think they are making bad calls. Try to remember that most officials are doing the best they can. Smart head coaches teach their players and assistant coaches to be respectful of the officials during a game. If you yell at them too much, they might become vindictive toward your team. The best rule for talking with officials is simple: only the head coach should do it. If an assistant coach wants to make a point to the officials, he should go to the head coach first. If the head coach thinks the point is important enough, he can approach the officials.

If a *player* wants to communicate with an official, he should go through his assistant coach. The only exception is if a player is a team captain on the field—in that case, he is allowed to approach the official in a respectful manner during a game.

All players and coaches must respect the field of play and stay within the established boundaries. Remember, it's okay to be excited when your team makes a great play. But inappropriate celebration will not be tolerated by the officials and will draw a penalty. Building good relationships with the officials is to your advantage, so try not to make them mad.

CHEER A GREAT PLAY!

I'm sure you've witnessed a baseball player hit one out of the park. Everyone jumps out of their seat and throws their arms up, going crazy for just a few minutes. Teammates jump around, congratulating each other, as they watch the batter round the bases and cross home plate, bringing the team closer to victory. Teammates understand that cheering a great play or a great hit is why we show up at the ballpark. It's fun! Great plays don't happen very often, but when they do, it's time to party. Cheer for your team as well as the great game of baseball! It's a special moment for everyone.

Remember, whether it's a great catch or a home run, be ready to cheer your team on and enjoy a special moment. This is a wonderful example from baseball, but it can happen in any sport.

DO THE RIGHT THING (SUMMER 1978)

If you're going to have a great program, your players need to trust each other in the locker room as well as on the field. I'm talking about taking equipment and personal property from each other. There's nothing more annoying than having a theft on the team.

I tell my players that if it happens, and we find out who is responsible, they're done, and no second chances. Doing the right thing is part of practicing leadership and being a winner. Thievery is a cancer to you and your team—get rid of it.

Here's a true story that happened years ago, and that I would refer to at the start of every season. Back when I was a young coach and teacher, barely making ends meet, I needed to take a part-time job. I would get up at 4 a.m. every morning, seven days a week, to deliver 400 newspapers by car, to support my wife and baby girl. After delivering the newspapers, I would race home, take a hot shower, and head to school to teach a full day of classes and coach.

One morning, I was driving along, delivering papers, and I came upon a beautiful little statue sitting on the side of the road, just a few feet up a dirt bank. It featured a boy with an umbrella, trying not to get rained on. I stopped my car and sat there looking at the statue for a minute or two. Then I got out, walked up the bank, and picked it up. I returned to my car, setting the statue in the back seat.

I was thinking how wonderful the statue would look on the front porch of our new house. I assumed someone had abandoned it, and I quickly drove off, thinking it would be all right for me to take it. I continued delivering my papers, but negative thoughts invaded my head, telling me the statue wasn't mine, and to take it back. Even though the statue had been sitting on the side of the road, and looked abandoned, I kept thinking I had taken someone else's property.

I drove on for a while, until for whatever reason, I swung the car around and headed back to where I'd found the statue. When I arrived, I stopped the car, grabbed the statue from the back seat, and quickly went up the bank, placing it back where I'd found it. Then I got in and drove off.

I immediately felt better. I was relieved. My thoughts drifted back on what had just happened. I thought about how I would have gotten back home and placed the statue on our front porch. From that moment on, I would have seen it every day coming home from work. It would be sitting there staring at me, reminding me how I'd acquired it, and how I had taken something that wasn't mine. Of course, my wife would have asked where the statue came from, and I would have needed to make up a story or maybe even tell her the truth about how I had taken it from the side of the road. She would have been upset, and we would never have enjoyed the statue, because it wasn't really ours. It would always have a dark cloud hanging over it.

At the start of every season, I would tell this story to my players, so they didn't mess with their teammates' equipment or personal property in the locker room. I wanted the players to clarify their thoughts about taking from their teammates. How would they feel afterward? How would they feel if something had been stolen from *them*? I wanted the team to understand how and why a theft on our team would cause an atmosphere of mistrust. Lastly, I would tell them to be smart about protecting personal property; I'd recommend not leaving it laying around. I always ended the story with encouragement to do the right thing.

BELIEVE IN YOURSELF

Believing in yourself is not always easy, especially when you're young and you haven't competed a lot. Seasoned athletes are talented and have learned over time and many competitions that they are good at what they do. They recognize their talent and nurture a passion to set goals and perform at an even higher level. Through dedication and hard work, they achieve their dreams.

As a young boy participating in many different sports, I had no idea that one day I would be competing in college, and later, that I'd compete as a high school coach. It all started when I received positive comments from people watching me play. These people helped me become aware of my ability to compete. Their feedback started me thinking that I might have some talent. My youth coach reinforced that idea by indicating that I was one of the best he had ever coached. His words opened my eyes to a new level of confidence. They also helped me love the game and work harder.

In high school, I was honored by making all-league, two years consecutively. This recognition gave me a reason to work hard and to keep playing in college. I look back at all those years of competing, which helped mold me into the person I am today. I was lucky to have had the chance to play. I found out that competing at a higher level is not without defeats along the way. It wasn't fun when I lost, but it taught me to enjoy winning more.

By the time I entered college, I had served in Vietnam, and even though I hadn't played for two years, I'd been thinking of playing the whole time, considering how I wanted to play and the example I wanted to set on the field. When I reported to college I was in the best shape of my life and strong as a bull. Sadly, three days later, during practice, I fell and broke my collar bone. Once again, I found myself getting knocked down, and starting all over. But I never gave up trying to achieve my dream.

Earning recognition and trying to achieve your dreams can be a long, difficult road. In college, I was still very young, but I had enough experience playing to know who I was as a player. If you'd asked me back then whether I was good, I'd have given you the same answer I'd give you now. I'd look you in the eye and say, "Yes, I'm a great competitor." Perhaps that sounds arrogant to you, but I've carried that confidence with me my whole life.

At the time, I believed I could have beaten anyone. Please understand that I'm older and wiser now. These days, I realize there's always someone better. It's good to believe in yourself on your journey in life, but remember, success is not free.

Remember: there's no shortcut to victory!

ANSWER A BAD PLAY WITH A GREAT PLAY!

Answering a bad play with a great play is the true mark of a champion in any sport. Sitting in the bleachers, I always look for the players who won't get down on themselves when they've made a bad play. You can see their determination to come back with great effort, and to even things up. This type of competitor is hard to beat and exciting to watch and cheer for.

Anyone who plays knows that errors will happen. How the player deals with that situation is important to his own mindset and to the rest of the team. Coming back with a great play after you've made a mistake can lift your team up and ignite the watching fans. Remember: in competition, there are many different variables. Your performances will be remembered and evaluated over time in terms of your hundreds of plays—not in terms of one or two mistakes.

To help avoid mistakes, make sure you're ready and alert during the game. Know the situation. And finally: practice, practice, practice. Believe that you can find a way to win, and you will!

TRUCK AND TRAILER FOR THE CHAMPIONSHIP (SUMMER 1971)

It's a hot summer evening in 1971, and I'm on the sidelines, coaching in the championship game of one of my Cedar Hills little-league teams. Coaching is how I earn extra cash in the summer to work my way through college.

It's the bottom of the seventh inning, and my team is up to bat, and there is one out. We have Neil, our biggest and strongest baserunner, on third, and Harry, our speedster, on second. The game is tied, and this is our last chance to win before going into extra innings.

The fans are cheering. We're having a hard time hitting the ball, and our two weakest hitters are coming to the plate. We need to do something, now! The only bright spot is that our two best baserunners are on the bases.

I decide to give the signal for our special play, the "truck and trailer." My players look at each other. They know what's coming. The pitcher starts his wind-up, and Harry, my baserunner on second, takes off for third. Neil, who is on third, just stands there, waiting for

Harry, who's headed his way at full speed. When Harry gets close to third, they both head for home; Harry is now riding Neil's coattails. The pitcher throws the ball to the catcher, who immediately comes out to block the plate. Neil slams into him and is tagged out as he knocks the catcher to the ground. The catcher can't get back up in time to tag Harry out, too, so Harry crosses the plate a moment later.

The crowd goes utterly quiet, waiting for the umpire's call on Harry's play. With a booming voice, the umpire calls out, "SAFE!" The crowd erupts. The other team looks at us in disbelief as we jump for joy and celebrate sweet victory. Once again, we've won the Cedar Hills Little League Championship.

I guess you had to be there to understand the importance of this game. My players were what you would call the "leftovers"; they weren't supposed to be that good. But I could tell you something wonderful about each one of them, and I could describe the support of their wonderful parents. I loved these moments—being in a situation where you had to lay it all on the line. We'd practiced that play over and over, knowing that someday we'd pull it out of our bag of tricks, and it would get us through.

One of the great memories of coaching that team was Harry's swimming pool. It gets hot in the summer and after a ball game the whole team would head over to Harry's house. His parents would fire up the barbeque and we'd have fun talking about the game while cooling off in the large pool in their back yard. After swimming and eating hamburgers for a couple of hours, we'd all head home, ready to do it all over again the next day. What a great way to spend the summer.

WATCHING THE OTHER TEAM

It's always good to watch the other team's warmup before a game to see if they work hard. How well do they use their fundamentals? What strengths do they have? Lazy and slow warmups send a message to me as a coach. I will be more aggressive if I think the other team is daydreaming. I will hold them accountable for not being prepared and put pressure on them to make plays.

Having said that, some teams and players can surprise you. They may look lazy and slow during warmup but reveal their abilities during the game. I always want to know the opposing team's roster and win/loss record before we play. I want to know who on their team can make the big plays. I can tell the real good teams by the way they carry themselves on and off the field. The great teams have great character and walk with confidence. They look for the coach to set the example.

Remember: there's no shortcut to victory. To be good, you must display great determination, sportsmanship, humility when victorious, and strength when defeated.

PS: Remember, the other team is watching you, too!

THE FROG ON THE TRACK (LATE SUMMER 1971)

The first day we reported for football practice at Linfield University, we all headed up into the stadium bleachers to wait for Coach Rutschman to give us the pre-season speech. Sitting there in the cool morning air, I looked to my left. Walking toward us on the track was a freshman named Steve Barsotti.

In high school, Steve had played defensive end for the Jesuit Crusaders. We found out very quickly that he was, to say the least, a little crazy. I guess he wanted to make a statement to the players sitting in the stands. As he approached, a frog hopped across the track in front of him. Without losing a step, he snatched it up, put its head in his mouth, and bit it off. He spit the head out on the track and threw the rest of the frog on the grass. Then he smiled at us and took a seat.

I couldn't believe what I had witnessed. This guy was different from the rest of us. Steve went on to be the starting defensive end for the Linfield Wildcats. He also became an All-American. Despite that first impression, he was a great guy. In 1971, we didn't think too much about why a kid like him would bite the head off a frog.

We were all kids, and sometimes young men do things that may not be regarded as appropriate. In hindsight, it was an appalling act of nineteen-year-old cruelty . . . but Steve really was a great kid. His character, as he matured, proved to be exemplary. We all admired him for the guy he *really* was, without the show-off actions of that first encounter.

Steve's other problem was that in the afternoons when we showed up for practice, he couldn't keep his eyes open for chalk talk. One day, Coach Rutschman got after him pretty good for dozing off while coach had his back turned and was drawing plays on the board. To avoid getting in trouble, Steve had hung the back of his football jersey on a coat hook behind him. This kept his head up, making it look like he was awake and paying attention.

Our other defensive end, Jay Buse, had also dozed off. When Rutschman saw both players sleeping, he stopped his chalk talk, grabbed a large silver garbage can next to the board, picked it up over his head with a crazed look, and slammed it down in front of both players.

Buse was so startled that his eyes opened wide, and he threw his elbow back against the wall behind him, knocking a two-foot-wide hole into it. Barsotti fell to the floor, ripping the coat hook out of the wall, and yelling in terror. Then, with a frightened look on his face, he lay on the floor, staring at Coach Rutschman.

The room got quiet, and we all focused on Coach Rutschman to see what would happen next. There was a long silence that seemed to last forever, and then everyone burst into laughter. It was a special moment. The rest of the season, when walking into the locker room, we'd see the patch on the wall where Buse had demonstrated his great strength. We'd notice the missing coat hook, and the place where Barsotti had been frightened to his knees. Both players will always be remembered for their unique personalities and their inability to stay awake during chalk talk.

A BOY NAMED JOE: WHY I COACHED FOOTBALL

This is a story about a boy named Joe. Joe was the youngest in a family of four boys, all very large. Joe's dad was 6'7", and a mountain of a man. Joe's brothers—Pete, Stan, and Willie—were just like their father; big, strong, and fast. All three played college and then pro football. When Joe became one of my ninth-grade students at Highland Park, he wanted to be like his big brothers and play football. Joe had a learning disability, but he made up for it with his sense of humor and enthusiasm.

During the school year, Joe helped me with a fundraiser by making a haunted house. We set up a fake operating room in the office of the boys' P.E. dressing room. Joe played a doctor operating on a patient who was lying on an operating table under a blue light. He used hamburger as bloody guts, and he also made an hour-long recording of himself imitating a heartbeat, using his own voice for the sound effect. He played the heartbeat recording as people walked by and looked through the window, watching him "operate." He would slowly turn and look at them, and then walk toward the door as if to grab one of them, like a mad scientist. It looked like the real thing! The haunted house made over two thousand dollars that night, and Joe was the big hit.

Joe's learning handicap prompted a tough discussion on whether it was safe for him to play football. As the head football coach, I could see his sadness at being told he couldn't play. At that time, we had two ninth-grade football teams. One was made up of bigger players and the other of smaller players. We did this to make the games safer and more competitive. After getting to know Joe, I thought that even though he was a tall kid, he would fit better with the smaller team, given his disability. Getting permission for him to play, and explaining to the staff why he should have the same opportunity to play as his brothers, was not easy.

When I finally had convinced the staff to allow Joe to try out for the team, I told him, and his eyes lit up. He walked around the school, proud that he was going to be a football player. When practice started, I kept a close eye on him and made sure he was practicing with players close to his ability.

The first time Joe was knocked down, during a blocking drill, he cried. He just lay there on the ground, weeping. I told all the players to move ten yards downfield, and I continued the drill. I told Joe that when he was done crying, the team would be downfield, and he could get up and get back in line. I added, "Welcome to football."

After a while, Joe got to his feet and got back in line for the drill. When it was his turn again, he got knocked down again. Again, he started to cry. So, I moved the team again. But this time, I didn't say a word. I was letting Joe decide whether he was going to play football or not.

He got up and got back in line. He was ready, once again, for his turn. This time, I told him that he needed to knock the whoop-tee-do out of the other player. You could see the determination in Joe's eyes. When the ball was hiked and the two players came together, Joe drove his opponent down the field by ten yards. The other players went crazy—cheering Joe on, then surrounding him, patting him on the back, and telling him what a great job he had done. Joe smiled from ear to ear. He never cried on the field again.

Joe went on to be the starting right tackle for the lightweight team, and he had a wonderful season. He was voted Most Inspirational Player by his teammates. He never played football again after that season, but we all knew the experience had changed him forever. Joe's family thanked me for all I had done.

In the spring, Joe became my baseball equipment manager. He did a tremendous job, while always wearing a big smile. I loved that guy!

PLAYING WITH CONFIDENCE: HE NEVER MISSED! (1969)

I know it sounds crazy for those of you who know me, but it's true: I was asked to play semi-pro basketball in Yokosuka, Japan, while serving in Vietnam.

My ship the *USS Mars* was home ported in Japan. Every few months, after going up and down the coast of Vietnam, we would head back to replenish our supplies and make repairs to the ship. While in port, I would spend my free time everyday playing pickup basketball games at the naval base gym. I was in tremendous shape, and not only from the basketball games. After playing, I would lift weights, trying to get stronger.

Back then, I loved basketball. Even though my dribbling wasn't the greatest, I could shoot—I mean, I could shoot the eyes out of the basket! Normally, in these pickup games at the gym, if you missed a shot, your team would lose. The competition was fierce. I wasn't the tallest player, so I had to shoot from way outside or try a jump shot from the corner.

One day, there was a strange man sitting in the bleachers watching the games. When I was done playing for the day, I headed for the weight room, and this guy stopped me and introduced himself as the head coach of the Yokosuka Hawks, which at that time was the town's semi-pro basketball team. I shook his hand, and he asked if I would like to play for the Hawks. I said, "Really?" He said, "Yes—I've watched you, and you don't miss."

I couldn't believe it. Back in high school I was number 15 on a JV team my junior year. I was really intrigued by the offer and told him I would give it a try. The next thing I knew (i.e., the next night!) I was sitting on the bench in full uniform at my first official game with this team. There was a large crowd in the arena. Incredible! Soon, the coach waved me over and said, "Geigle, check in."

Finally, I thought, *someone sees my true talent in basketball!*

I check in and immediately get the ball. I dribble down the floor and pass the ball off. Then it comes back to me, and I shoot. The ball goes completely over the backboard. The crowd groans, letting me know they're not pleased. With that, my confidence goes right out the window.

A short time later, the coach took me out. My first appearance hadn't earned me a lot of respect. I thought I didn't belong with these guys; I needed to be back in the gym, playing rat ball. After the game, I told the coach I didn't feel comfortable and would be better off playing for fun. That was my total experience of playing semi-pro. But I did go on to become a talented gym rat!

Thinking about it now, I regret having given up so easily. Maybe I would have settled down, and my shooting might have returned.

LARRY MCJURY, WONDER BOY

After I got out of the service and had become a teacher, I made extra money on the weekends as a gym supervisor for a recreation center in Beaverton, Oregon. I watched and supervised the athletes who came in to play pick-up basketball.

Without a doubt, some tremendous talent came through that door. On occasion, players from the Portland Trailblazers would come in and play with their buddies, just for fun. My favorite player was a tall young Black athlete by the name of Larry McJury. He was fast and aggressive, and he could shoot the ball from just about anywhere. I loved this guy, not only as a player, but as a friend.

Larry would come down the floor dribbling the basketball. He'd smile, telling the other team the game was over. Then he'd step over the half-court line (yes, the *half-court line*), set up for a jump shot, and shoot the ball from the cheap seats. When it came down, it was all net. He would then look at the other team and say, "Game over! Next!" That would intimidate the next five guys who were going to play his team.

Larry was just a flat-out great guy. I'll never forget him. He must have seen something in me that he liked; he always treated me well. Sometimes we would see each other in a shopping mall or somewhere else. He'd always say hello and we'd talk for awhile. Maybe he respected my ability to supervise and control the gym. Games got competitive, and sometimes fights or arguments broke out, and I had to do my job. I let the players know that if they didn't stop when I told them to, they would be kicked out. There were a few times I had to call the police to really get their attention. If I did that, you were banned from the gym permanently.

Maybe Larry respected me because I was tough and didn't back down, even though these guys were bigger and stronger. I continued to supervise the gym for a long time and played pick-up basketball there for many years. Now that I'm retired, I don't play anymore. But I still remember those days in the gym, playing and watching the wonder boy!

Always remember: play with confidence.

I WANTED TO BE A WILDCAT

I thought I would share how hard I had to work to play football at Linfield. Later, as a coach, I always searched for players who not only had skill but were motivated and willing to work hard. That work ethic, I felt, was important to win.

With me, it started back as a young kid, working around the house. My father traveled a lot and was gone for weeks at a time. When he came home, I'd spend hours working to keep the yard up, just to hear him say, "Great job." I carried those two words with me my whole coaching career.

In the summers, I spent hours with the neighborhood kids playing basketball, street football, and baseball. By the time I started competing in school sports, I knew what hard work was. My drive carried over to games—playing hard and not giving up. Years later, I used that same motivation to play football at Linfield University, after serving sixteen months in Vietnam. I didn't know it at the time, but I was suffering from PTSD, from a fall I had taken aboard my ship, the USS Mars. The Linfield University part of my story happened in the summer of 1971.

Getting Ready for Football, Summer 1971

Because I was not going to let my dreams of playing for Linfield pass me by, my workouts for football were regular and tough. I worked at a health club and used the weight room every day to get stronger. I received summer letters from Linfield and learned what would be expected of me in the fall. At that time, Coach Rutschman asked his players to be in great shape. We had to run ten 240-yard, timed sprints. Each sprint needed to be under thirty-five seconds, with just one minute rest between them. When I arrived, not only could I run all ten sprints—I had mastered twenty-two, all in under thirty-five seconds.

Knowing how important this football opportunity was, I couldn't sleep on my first night at Linfield. While everyone else was in bed, I went out to the football field, with a flashlight and stopwatch, and ran the ten 240s under time in the moonlight. At 8:00 a.m. the next morning, I did it all over again at the first practice with the football team. I was strong, fast, and ready to be a Wildcat.

It only took me three days to become the starting nose guard for Linfield. I went 100 percent every day in every practice. The coaches were happy with my performance, and they could see my desire to play.

About a week into practices, we were running sprints, when I fell and hurt my shoulder. Despite the pain, I kept going hard in practice until Coach Rutschman called me over and asked why I was favoring my right side. I told him I had fallen during sprints. He told me to have a doctor check it out.

When I saw the doctor, he gave me some bad news: I had a broken collarbone and couldn't play for six weeks. Though I was disappointed, I kept doing what I could to stay in shape. Six weeks later, I was once again ready to go, excited to play in my first game as a Wildcat. I remember the team loading out in front of the stadium, where the bus was waiting. We were headed to play at Pacific University, in Forest Grove, Oregon. Just before I stepped on the bus, Coach Rutschman said he needed to talk with me. He told me that Pacific University had just called to say I was half a credit short, and not eligible to play this season.

You can't imagine the disappointment I felt after all the hard work I had done to get ready. I couldn't believe Pacific would take the time to check my transcripts. Coach Rutschman told me he would honor my athletic grant and work-study, and he would redshirt me for the 1971 season. So, I continued to attend Linfield for the rest of 1971.

During the school year I went on to meet some great people, and after many hours of talking with friends and professors, I decided I'd become a teacher and coach after graduating from Linfield. This was an important decision, and it gave me the direction I needed to be successful and to help others. I had just made it through my first year at Linfield and had not lost my dream of playing football for the Wildcats. Because of Ad Rutschman and Linfield University, I was on my way to helping thousands of young people over a thirty-year career in education and coaching.

Back on the Field (1972)

In 1972 I worked even harder to get ready for fall and to make the team once again. I was hell-bent on being the starting nose guard.

Even though my accident on board the USS *Mars* was affecting me and my relationships with others, I worked hard on the football field and found the distraction helpful. I had a good first two weeks of practice, and once again I was made the starting nose guard.

On September 16 the Wildcats traveled to Central Washington University. That was a special day for me. It was my first football game since 1968. Not only was I back—I was back big-time. I was well-prepared because I'd watched game film against Central Washington. I made sixteen unassisted tackles, with an additional eight assisted tackles, for a total of twenty-four tackles in a single game. According to the unofficial records, that is the most tackles in a single game in the history of Linfield football. The following Monday, I was praised by the coaches, picked as the "Top Cat of the Week," and interviewed by the *Oregonian*. Without a doubt, that was the best game I ever played.

Our next game was September 23, against the Portland State Vikings. We played this one at Linfield, in the mud. Both Central Washington and Portland State were in a higher division, and both were favored to beat us. Once again, I played well. I had a total of sixteen tackles in the mud, along with at least two fumble recoveries. We lost 6-0, but the team played well, and I was having a lot of fun.

Game three, against Pacific University, was on September 30. I was hit hard in the upper right leg and didn't see action in the fourth quarter. Even though I didn't play in the fourth quarter, for that game I still managed to rack up four unassisted tackles, four assisted tackles, two quarterback sacks, two forced fumbles, and two fumble recoveries. I was still hell-bent for leather, playing hard and knocking people around. I was healthy and playing well.

The hit to my right leg put me on the bench against Whitman College on October 7, but I returned against Willamette on October 14. Even though my leg wasn't one hundred percent, I acted like it was, so I could play. I never was good at standing and watching. I needed to be *in* the game. On October 14, against Willamette University, I made eight tackles, two quarterback sacks, one quarterback hurry, and one forced fumble. My leg held up, but it wasn't quite healed yet. Also, I noticed that being out during the previous week had made me tired.

The next week during practice, my leg was acting up. So, I didn't practice all week, and didn't play against the College of Idaho on October 21. I was disappointed. I could feel myself getting weaker and weaker as I missed practice. I knew that to play my best football, I needed to be at full strength. With my injury, I couldn't run, and I couldn't lift weights with my bad leg.

Our next game was on October 28, against Lewis & Clark College. I suited up but played less than half the game. I seemed a step slower and somewhat weaker. I managed four tackles, one forced fumble, and one quarterback hurry. I wasn't upset, but I knew why my playing ability was diminished. I was not in the physical shape I needed to be in to compete, and it was showing.

Our next game wasn't until November 11, against Pacific Lutheran University, which was always our strongest rival. I thought that would be enough time to heal and gain some strength back. But it just wasn't meant to be.

I ended up getting very sick with a bad virus. My anxiety was acting up, and I was having panic attacks, without knowing why. It scared me a lot. I was sick as a dog for almost two weeks, with a fever and chills. I needed to get better and get back on the field. I went to see the doctor. He put me on penicillin, which I immediately had an allergic reaction to—and that brought my panic attacks to a new level. Sometimes I felt like I couldn't breathe. My stomach was always upset. In class at Linfield, I would need to get up and leave. I was scared, and I couldn't figure out why I was so obsessed with my physical condition.

I got to a point where the virus was gone, but the after-effects of my anxiety remained. And there was something more going on with me. Something that I didn't understand, but that wasn't going away.

When I returned to practice, I was weak, and not the same. The defensive coach thought I was being lazy, so he sent me over to the ropes to run by myself, and to make me feel bad. When Coach Rutschman saw me, he called me over and asked what I was doing at the ropes. I told him, and he told me to go back with the team. It never came up again, and the defensive coach had a different attitude the next day. I believe Coach Rutschman knew I was not quite myself. He also knew I was not lazy.

On November 11, 1972, we played Pacific Lutheran University. I suited up, and only played for a short while in the first quarter. I think it was payback by the defensive coach. I came to realize he was a kind of a jerk. He probably thought I got him in trouble with Coach Rutschman, and he limited my time on the field as punishment. He was the first Linfield football coach I didn't care for, and the only person at Linfield who I felt didn't belong there. I guess he didn't know me or my love of the game very well.

Next, we were scheduled to play the University of Hawaii. This was to be our final game. I didn't think I would be picked to go, but I was doing better in practice and made the traveling squad. I was still on medication when we arrived in Hawaii and suited up for our first practice.

During that practice, I started to feel funny. My stomach just wouldn't settle down. I told Coach Rutschman, and asked if I could borrow a dollar to go across the street to McDonald's and get a vanilla milkshake. He gave me a strange look, then pulled out a dollar and handed it to me. I hustled across the street and stood in the ordering line in full practice gear.

By the time I returned to the field, I had downed the shake. I rejoined the practice. Five minutes later, I was on the sideline, lying on the bench—shaking, red-faced, and flushed. The coaches rushed me to the hospital in the back of a rental car. When we pulled up outside the emergency room, they had me lay down on a park bench outside the hospital so the doctor could examine me there. He looked at me, checked a few things, and then asked, "Are you on any medication?" I nodded. Then he asked me to try and calm down. He told me he thought I was having a panic attack.

As he spoke, I started to calm down and started feeling better. He thought that I had taken the medication too long, and it had killed all the good bacteria in my system, and when I started feeling bad it set off the panic attack. He told me not to take any more medication, and to eat plenty of cottage cheese and yogurt to replenish the good bacteria in my body. By the time he was done talking, I had calmed down. I sat up, and a little while later got back in the car and headed for the hotel. The next few days, I felt a lot of anxiety, being so far away from home. But I got through practice and made it to game night.

Hawaii was also a division higher than Linfield and was picked to win. Even though we had won our league championship, we were no match for the Islanders. I played but was not very effective. I was glad when the game was over. After the game, we headed for the airport. On the plane, I had a seat to myself and slept the whole flight. I was happy that we were back home, and that I had finished my first full season as a Linfield Wildcat. I attended classes the rest of the year, looking forward to the next football season and a chance to heal up and get stronger again.

Faith

One of the great programs on campus during my time at Linfield was the Fellowship of Christian Athletes. Time and time again I would observe these athletes, and their actions and friendships on campus. It appeared to me that their faith was in every aspect of their life, but especially on the football field. I found myself drawn to and inspired by them.

Becoming a Christian Athlete changed my whole perspective on why I was playing football. It gave me a renewed spirit and direction. I wanted to play football for the right reasons—for my faith, my team, my parents, and my community. At that time, I loved what was good in the world—not what other people thought was good, but truths that had come from centuries of trial and error. Truths that were as true as they had been hundreds of years before. When I read the Bible, I tried to identify as many of these truths as I could, so I could implement them in my life.

One Sunday during football season, I was in church, sitting

with a group of friends, listening to the pastor's stories about faith and inspiration. Suddenly, he turned and looked right at me. Out of the blue, he started talking about how he had attended Linfield's football game the day before. He spoke about how this one player on Linfield's team was so inspiring to him—how he loved his effort and enthusiasm on the field. As the pastor spoke, he was animated and fired up. Then he indicated that this player was here in the church, sitting in the congregation. He went on to say what a pleasure it was, having nose guard Larry Geigle attending, and how much fun it had been to watch him on the football field.

After that, he went on with the rest of his sermon. I will never forget that day in church; it was better than any football victory!

Today, I feel the same about my faith. I love the true lessons of life and know there is no way anyone can live up to all of them. That doesn't mean we stop trying. I've seen what is good and right in this world, and it comes from doing the right thing. I really believed back then that people should live their lives by example, not empty words.

I found wonderful examples of great people at Linfield, on and off the field. The great ones didn't talk much but spoke loudly with their actions around campus and on the football field—for example, when they helped an opposing player off the ground after knocking the whoop-tee-do out of them.

I have purposely avoided talking about the impact of my accident on the *USS Mars*, and how it affected me during my college days. Though my PTSD was present at Linfield, I never understood how it affected my performance and consistency. This was the 70s, and PTSD was not fully understood or even acknowledged. You were supposed to "suck it up" and be tough. But it's a strange condition. I have paid a dear price for an accident that happened when I was nineteen. Looking back, I can honestly say that the accident on the USS *Mars* had a dramatic influence on my college performance, and my ability to trust, feel safe, and be secure. Not only was the trauma still present, but it continued to expand its influence in my life and would do so forever.

Linfield (Fall 1973)

I stayed at Linfield during the summer before my third year, taking classes so I could graduate early. That cut my time in college down to three years. 1973 would be my final football season. Once again, I had worked hard to be a Wildcat. My faith and confidence had grown. I was rested, physically healthy, and strong as a bull.

Back on the Field (1973)

After my final summer camping trip, it was time to play football. I was happy to be back on the field. I quickly won the starting nose guard position, and after a few weeks of practice, we were ready for our first game against Portland State, on September 22, at the Civic Stadium in Portland.

It was a rainy day, and the Portland State field had artificial grass—although back then it looked more like living-room carpet than grass. We had Portland State's number that year, and we won 19-3. Coach Rutschman was happy with our performance. I walked away with ten tackles and one forced fumble.

The following week, on September 29, we won against Whitworth College. I was flying high with fifteen tackles and another fumble recovery. I picked up a fumbled ball and ran fifteen yards before getting tackled. Then, on October 6, we beat Willamette University at Linfield. I blocked a punt, forced a fumble, and made three tackles. The fourth game into the season was played on October 13, against the College of Idaho. I turned in thirteen tackles and another forced fumble.

Playing college nose guard at 190 pounds dripping wet can get a little rough. The next week, against Lewis & Clark, I was coming down the field on a kickoff, and slammed my right hand into the helmet of an opposing player. My hand was broken, but I didn't know it at the time. The injury made me mad. The very next play, when the ball was hiked, I gave a forearm to the center—and once again, I was in pain. When I got off the field, the team doctor grabbed me and had a look at my hand. He told me I was done playing—he thought that my hand was broken in three places. He also said that if I went back in the game, he would have to operate to wire my hand back together. So that was it for me for the season—and, since it was my last year at Linfield, for football.

We lost that game to Lewis & Clark, 7-4. Coach Rutschman let us know how unhappy he was on the way back to Linfield.

The next four weeks went by slowly, but finally the season was over. Once again, we were league champions of our conference. After all the league selections were announced and I didn't receive any honors, I stopped by Coach Rutschman's office and asked him if I had received any votes for all-league. He thought for a moment, and then said, "I think you got one vote."

I was disappointed that for all my hard work I had only received one vote. I thought later that maybe I tried too hard, wearing myself down until I became injured and sick. If I had stayed healthy and not missed so many games, I would have received the votes and recognition I deserved. I said goodbye to Linfield football, focusing on graduating in the spring and receiving my teaching certification.

Throughout my career, I made many sacrifices, over and over, but I never gave up on my dream. I will always be a Linfield Wildcat!

Thank you, Coach Rutschman.

THE BIG TAKEOVER (1966-67)

This story is taken from my book Coach Bear 30 (The Life and Times of Coach Larry Geigle) *which was the first book I wrote about my life. I wanted my children to know their father as a young boy. The setting is my junior year of high school, playing football at Sunset High School, in Beaverton, Oregon, for Mouse Davis. I had made the varsity team the year before as a sophomore and lettered. This year I had decided to take over the starting fullback and nose guard positions. I was not going to be denied and was determined to prove to Mouse that I had arrived.*

When the 1967 football season rolled around, I was ready for "the big takeover." Sometime during the previous school year, I had decided to become the starting fullback *and* nose guard.

The first few days of practice were crucial for me to win those positions. My moment came on the second day of practice, when we were running plays. Everyone thought Frank Fortino would be the next fullback. He was a senior, and it was his turn. Coach called a scramble-right pass, where the fullback blocks the defensive end. Frank's team ran the play first, and his block was average and not that impressive. Then it was my team's turn to run the same play. The ball was hiked, and I headed for the defensive end at full speed. When I arrived, I knocked down the defensive end with what soon became known as the famous "Geigle Forearm."

You could hear the groans from the other players when the defensive man went down and didn't get up for a while. The coaches looked at each other. They didn't say much, but I could see their expressions. Coach Davis then told me to change teams. He called for a fullback off-tackle play, and I was to get the ball. I don't know what got into me, but when I got the ball, I ran down the field for forty yards, with players trying to tackle me. I either dodged them or ran right over them, like I was some sort of prehistoric animal looking for my next meal.

Once again, the coaches didn't say anything. But I knew I had done the job, and the "little fat boy" was gone forever. The next day I was moved to the starting unit and became the team's starting fullback and nose guard.

I'll never forget that year. We became such a good football team. Coach Davis would give me the ball on that off-tackle play over and over. One night in the pouring rain, I ran like a plow horse for 175 yards in the mud, in a game against Centennial High School. I received the game ball from Coach Davis. It was a great night for our team.

I couldn't help thinking I was starting to become a good fullback, and I was very proud. At the end of the season, I was the leading scorer for Sunset High. But when the all-league selections came out, to my surprise, I was selected second team all-league on *defense*, not offense. On defense, I had led the team in tackles and had become a tough nose guard—but I loved fullback so much that I hadn't really thought about how I was playing as a nose guard.

Shortly after the league selection came out, I started receiving recruitment letters—they came from the University of Oregon, Oregon State, the University of Washington, and Washington State. Later, I received an invitation to Oregon State for their spring scrimmage to meet the coach and players and have lunch. I attended, of course. After watching the Beavers' scrimmage, I was invited into the locker room to meet some of the players. I was blown away by their size. When I left, I thought I might be too small to play division one football.

The big takeover was the start of my time being first team. I remained starting nose guard and fullback for the next two years, until graduation. And I was voted "all league" for 1967 and 1968.